The Spectrum of Love

AF623655

Nam

BookLeaf Publishing

Presentation by *BookLeaf Publishing*

Web: www.bookleafpub.com

E-mail: info@bookleafpub.com

ISBN: 9789357213080

First edition 2023

The End

It's not a good feeling when you're forced to question the things you believed all your life. I think that's a part of life to some degree, the way life humbles you as you get your foot in the door of adulthood. Everything about the way love raised you up until this point, and then your cut loose to be the king of your own perception, and it's almost comical during this stage to realize the ways you were naive. You spend a decade building a nest egg of routine and then one day it's like everything you took to build what peace you have no longer applies to the tomorrow we face. Evolution is something that's always fascinated me, the natural progression of man and how far we've come. I can't help but think this particular chapter be the beginning of the end though. It makes me sad how frequent these thoughts have been coming in and out of my days. You never realize how good home is until you find yourself not having one. There's not much worse than not being able to grow towards the vision of how you thought life was supposed to be. And it makes it worse when that was supposed to be this chapter, but you're worried about where your home will be tomorrow. It brings the value of love to the surface to reminisce on a prior chapter when we took these things for granted. We can see the way love gives us strength to dream; to create a vision at all. From desire, that's rooted from the percetion we blindly inherited of the path we were told of how to live this life. There's a world all around me, people passing me by with some where to go. Places to be. Everyone in route-- Somewhere they belong. And here I am, wishing I could just go home, but wishing that is longing for a past chapter, a place that no longer exists. And I don't seem to belong anywhere, to anyone, and my days are made up of fighting off how paralyzing that sadness has become. But it doesn't matter how sad you are. It doesnt matter the tears you cry. Eventually they stop. They dry. And you move on just as ghostly as you once were.

The internet changed the game in alot of ways no one was prepared for. I remember being a child on New Year's Eve of 1999. Hearing someone say that this is when the computers shut the world down. No different than any farfetched science fiction, but that thought keeps surfacing in my mind as the timeline of existence unravels. The internet brought to life a new chapter of evolution. We can look at the invention of light, and transportation in the same manner. The ways they opened up the gateway of endless opportunities. In this particular instance, the convenience now shifts to the ability to do everything that was once needed, behind a screen that we call a phone that goes everywhere with us in our pockets. When I was 12 I can remember it started out as what they called instant messaging. The internet wasn't quite used like it is today, where we can find the answer to literally any question or curiosity we may have. It seems harmless, and maybe even just immature, the relationships you kindled online that you couldn't sustain when it came time to be face to face, because you could not articulate feelings in the same way as you could behind a screen. Fast forward two decades and the evolution of the internet progressed from a computer we sit at after our days would be over, to the readily accessible mobile devices that we wouldn't ever go anywhere without. We once wrote letters, and now we write thoughts, shared with our social circles at any impulse. The instant gratification it has subliminally instilled and how it slowly erodes the meaning of actual interaction. It's robbing us of our interpersonal communication skills as we slowly build these walls around us that we can't even see.

Maturing means Friction

You knew it was important to grow in each chapter, but growth was more like panic in my eyes. And you never really know the ways we need love until its too late. It's always in hindsight that love reveals itself. But even the times it's nowhere to be found, the love of what you believed was enough to guide you when you needed strength. You don't learn that until you leave home for the first time though. All the things you took for granted, turn to jolts of pain, every time the present hurts because of what existed in a past chapter. We'll call this a tragedy, and I've watched people build the grandest of walls in silence because of it. I am people. And I can't help but feel the sadness in all the people around me who have built these walls that I hope will not evolve into the pain that I have felt. But some of them will.

We get by in the first city because of the love that still blankets us from where we come from. And not just in the first city, but all the chapters our heart will hold onto strength in the memories we trace without knowing. We don't always understand, because very rarely are we forced to hurt enough that we have to dissect those memories for answers. Everything instilled from the place we call home is what propels us each chapter. And the more places you go, the more the depths of love will come to life, reminding you of where you come from. The ways that love protects and inspires us as we age the timeline. To grow old and alone is dangerous for the heart. And so, if this were the end, I'd want this to be a time capsule for anyone who might stumble upon footsteps like my own

I know that love wasn't always dark. I can at least recognize the bias from my own perspective, without it. I can't help but observe the patterns of how I struggle, and the delayed ways that society follows. I wish it were wrong, but those uncanny moments in your mind that no one but you knows. It comes from value, and slowly how the virtual world creeps up on that list without us batting an eye. It's when our heart grows from home and nothing is there to protect us. If this is true, I'd only want to leave advice for those that these words resognates with. When it comes down to it, honestly, love is everything. I never intended for time to blow my appreciation away like this. And so it's important I leave these trail of words for the future that may struggle. The way that life unravels before we're forced to wake up from all the ways we're influenced. That's how it seems at least. Or the ways the present moment comes to life when we learn regret for the first time. I never knew the ways that love was protecting me. I don't think that many people do. The ways we take love for granted. It's not until you sit in solitude with survival, or broken and by yourself that love from a past chapter will come to life. Those aren't things we're ever really taught growing up though. To understand beauty from a chapter after it is gone is to understand pain. No one prepares you for the ways your heart can bring you to your knees. I've learned that is when God makes himself visible though. I had to be so broken and alone, that I had no choice but to own all the wrong turns that lead me here. The mistakes we didn't know we were making. And it doesn't matter anymore at that point. Everything from the past, is the past. There's nothing worse than questioning if the love was real that we wanted to last forever. A lot of growing up is learning to remove the beliefs that we inherited blindly. And as time goes on, the chains we wear of our haunted subconscious. The things we believed in false perspective. The wrongs we did that no one knew but us, eventually will find their way back as silent jolts of pain to the heart. And hopefully there aren't so many mysteries that keep us up at night, that we can embrace tomorrow knowing who we are and the world around us. That we can trust our intuition, and of all the things we've seen and learned, it's important that we have hope now, and confidence in what is right, and good. To know God, and goodness, and all the ways we struggled and suffered up until this point, were for him.

Seeds of Love that turn to Roots

I first learned about love as a young child. I wish I could say it was in the same manner the kids around me grew up seeing. I learned the value of family seeing the ways my mother grew up as an orphan. The things I was neglected of would come to life at each chapter as what I would yearn for would teach me lessons of my empty past. The love she never had, and how that affected the way she mother'd me. We all have the opportunity to learn about love, as love will present itself to us, but the understanding never comes until later in life though. And some people go through their entire lives never caring to think about it. A chapter of solitude and pain, left with nothing other than memories to trace is where I feel I woke up. I wish there was a way other than pain to bring these lessons to life, there's not. Only to believe full heartedly from the start, but that also aligns with believing blindly. And that's ok as long as it's protected through life. But in the absence of love to protect us, those beliefs are bound to crumble. I practiced writing my feelings everyday for an entire winter in solitude, believing that if I could express the feelings I had inside, I would never be alone again. Sometimes it makes my heart smile how naive and driven I was. Sometimes it makes me cry too. Each person's perception of love starts with the very environment that raises us. The ways our mother is loved, and how she shines to the world is what sets the foundation, in ways we'll never even be able to verbalize. A new chapter will begin when our heart aligns those dots with the world we see around us. When we look back on our lives we can see the chapters we are naive. The chapters our judgement and clarity are distorted by the things we value. The things we haven't experienced. I suppose that's why childhood is considered a gift, our ability to dream before life builds our walls.

I used to resent my mother because of the struggles we had and how they made me different. Looking back, I don't think it was the struggles that made me different. And if I'm being honest, I think the struggles are what contributed to any chance of greatness I ever had. But I never truly understood the ways I was different until 30 years into life. Growing up as a kid, I never believed I was different. I was the only non white kid at recess in a small town with less than 1,000population, but that never made me feel any different at all. One thing I've learned about growing up is that we naturally take out our frustration on the people closest to us. I think ultimately, that's what builds the bond within a family, is the ways we grow through time, going through adversity. The anchor that it instills and the value that it has in keeping love alive. And in ways we never really learn to verbalize. Another thing I learned is the ways we're forced to mature. But the thing about maturing is, it doesn't take place without friction. And this is where the value of love skyrockets in its ability to nurture that growth. Because without it is only to accelerate the ways we feel alone. I didn't learn about this until I had the opportunity to feel like a father though, and the ways love naturally poured from my heart in all the ways I needed when I was a child. Almost as if my life had prepared me to be the father I would always want, but before I could grow into the man I needed to be. and when I say father, I might as well say King, and Queen, in the roles we have in how a child's heart will grow. All the times I can remember the way my mother's words would bring me to my knees. Nothing was ever good enough for her. She was not impressed very often, but the more I age the more I naturally align with her footsteps. And to move anywhere without what protected me seems impossible alone. The ways her words could crumble me in any moment. And when I say crumble, the same way you'd collapse to your knees in tears. And that vision would look exactly the same in and out of every chapter of my life. The only thing that got better was my ability to keep my feelings to myself. It took me a long time to even admit the idea of being sensitive. That's not something a man in a small town is ever proud of being. The ways my heart attached to the most random scenes of life; anything at all, a father holding his child's hand walking down the sidewalk. A child with old and beat up sneakers. Could be a tree I was grateful for in passing. How any random vision of present life could be the domino effect of something much greater. It could be anything, and the process to understanding, accepting, and being able to articulate these scenes took nearly 20 years in itself to be able to recognize and understand. But it got to a certain point I knew it wasn't like the people around me. I built walls to keep those feelings safe. I learned to recognize the potential onset of those feelings, in any scenario, so that I could avoid and protect myself from them. Little did I know, these were feelings I was masking that held a lot of truth for understanding. And by the time I was learning these things, I had built so many walls around me that I found myself alone. A road that took me on a different path, through a handful of cities that left me alone with no one there. and hurting, when I needed to be protected the most.

The Wind Blows

The third city was was the first time I was entirely alone, but where I grew the most. The gulf of Mexico, a small little tourist city called Panama City Beach, Florida. I had 200$, a place to live, and a job, working as a professional beach photographer. In hindsight, it was honestly one of the best business models I had ever seen, not that I had known or understood anything about business at the time. Running up and down the beach, talking to every single person on your stretch of sand. This was one of the chapters that would shape me the most. Where I felt and saw things that I wouldn't want anyone to see or feel, but I'm grateful for the lessons it gave me. When you think about running up and approaching someone on the beach it sounds kinda terrifying, but I never knew this was something you could be trained for. Identifying the target demographic. Was it a married couple? Was it a group of kids on senior week? A family? That would determine how you broke the ice, and since you knew everyone was on vacation, that made it easy. I learned that there were only so many directions the conversation could go, and when it came down to it, who wouldnt want professionally captured pictures of the people they're closest with while on vacation. Not to mention, Panama City was beautiful! There wasn't very many waves being on the gulf, and the water was crystal blue on most calm days. You could trace forever to the horizon and the blue sky would bring you back to the beauty of how a small wave would crash. It wasn't out of the question to see manatees, dolphins, sharks, manta rays...

That wasn't even the best part. We lived in a 3story mansion all together. And every day each person would invite groups back to the house. I know it sounds crazy, but honestly, it was crazier. I'm glad for the close quarters that the living arrangement forced us all to be in, because that's ultimately what allowed me to find any comfort at all. One of my best friends for life came out of this chapter. One of the best captains on the water, and he'd joke about the times I would try to go out and party with them only to end up dissapearing to walk home alone when I felt too uncomfortable. I was always kind of socially awkward and shy, but being an athlete all my life is something that also kept me from not being an outcast. The way I physically looked is something I was reminded that had value, and when it comes down to it, that couldn't be any more true.

The owners of the photography company had specifically picked this place out. We were the new guys on the beach, and what gave us an advantage was that most of us had already worked for the owners in Ocean City, Maryland. They had took a business model that already existed and came somewhere where that business would thrive. There was a company called aquatic adventures that ran parasails out in front of each stretch of beach. It was incredible! There was a deckhand and captain on the boat, they'd drive by each hotel with a parachute attached up in the sky. Heights is something that I've always been terrified of but I remember the first day they made me strap up and sent me up in the air. Like a peaceful float, sitting on a swing in the middle of the clouds. To be eye level with the sky you'd watch connect to the horizon from down on the sand was incredible. Then there was a shuttle captain that drove a jetski with a banana boat on the back that held a dozen or so passengers. And on the beach, there were huts where the beach boys would sign people up and set out chairs for the guests at each hotel. Everyone worked as a team together to make this business work. All of these workers were resident locals to the beach, and what fascinated me was how much they resembled in character the people from that poor town in Pennsylvania that I had come from. It was the furthest from a city, and there were definitely no beaches around. Not really any experiences at all other than work and time you spent with your family growing up. It was so intriguing to me the resemblance these locals had of the people of where I had come from, except, the ones who wore boots and hunted from my poor little town, were the same ones that wore boardshorts and flip flops with racoon eyes from wearing sunglasses all day on the boat. What made it even more fascinating, was the way that growing up in a tourist city shaped the societal norms of these people.

March kicked off the start of the tourist season, and it was spring break. One week it would be Penn State, Ohio State, Wisconsin, Minnesota. The next week would be Texas, Auburn, Georgia. And then Harvard, Stanford, Cornell. Every week, a new crowd of different faces. But what was also fascinating was that the conversations were the same. The intent was the same. It was entirely different people from different walks of life, just having the same interactions.

What You do When No One Sees, Matters

It was around this time that someone from a rival school back home had reached out to me. He was the son of a Dr. and we had grew up having mutual interests and knowing each other from sports. Little did I know that this is what would change my life forever. Looking back, he knew I was a perfect target. But I couldn't turn him down, I was just a boy mentally, but developed enough to be able to handle the proposition. What I describe next would layout the basis of every underground steroid operation throughout the United States.

There were online forum boards that die hard gym rats and bodybuilders would go to to talk about everything under the sun that had to do with bodybuilding, fitness, food, training, everything.... A forum board was an online community where people could talk about things of illegal nature. Things they couldn't talk about with people in everyday life. Not all forum boards are like this, but the ones that we were on were. There were people called moderators that would oversee the chatrooms and group discussions, but it was also a place to buy illegal anabolic steroids. People would post reviews of their experiences with different labs and it was a way for people who had the same interest in bodybuilding to be able to get their hands on these illegal substances. I never really understood it so I didn't bother to spend time on them. All i knew was that when there was an order, my friend, who I will call "Dom" for the sake of keeping his name anonymous. He would send me the order, the name, the address, and it was on me to package that up and take to the post office. At the time, I did not think of it as the one taking the risk. When he had reached out to me, I was excited just because I knew him as the cool kid from a rival school. I had told one of the roommates in the house who was also a gym rat and he had told me it was something I couldn't not do! I will reference him as "Jake" and Jake was one of the coolest kids in the house. He was wild! And when I say wild, he had an obnoxious way of keeping everyones attention, no matter where we were. He was a Maryland state champ in wrestling and we were best friends. It made me feel cool being close to him, and it was easy to not say much always being by his side. He would do things like try to sneak into the bedroom when someone was hooking up with a girl. I've seen him dump a beer over a girl's head who turned him down. Looking back, he was not a very a good person. But we were all kids, and he had a way about him that everyone always wanted to be around him. And being his best friend, I went everywhere with him. I let him help me with orders, and eventually Dom would send down all the supplies needed to make, store, and ship out these steroids that were bought through online forums. When I talk about the naivety of life, I guess this could be a prime example. I knew it was illegal but how he described the process of what I needed to do and knowing no one needed to know but me, somehow made me think it was ok. I was manufacturing, packaging, and shipping illegal steroids throughout the country. It wasn't anything that I was proud of deep down, but Jake had a way of making it seem awesome. And we made enough money to not have to stress, to be able to do the things we wanted, and everyone wanted to be around us.

It eventually got so big that I had to get my own place. And that's when things kinda went downhill. I did not know how good it was for me to have roommates. Being alone, I ended up just isolating myself when the tourist season was over. The town was ghostly in the offseason and I realized that I didn't really make any real friends at all. A dark lonliness creeped over me from summer and I found myself more alone than I had ever been in my life. Knowing that I was doing illegal things built these walls around me that kept anyone from ever getting to know me. I was trapped. I say this is where I learned to talk because I would spend my days practicing writing my feelings. Writing anything really. To pass the time. To not hurt. I didn't plan on spending a season writing my feelings but it gave me a new found ability to be able to speak in ways that I never could before. I remember I went almost two months without any interaction at all. And that's not anything any person should ever experience. I was so lonely that the people who worked at the post office loved seeing me. And I loved seeing them. Not only was it the only kindness I saw in my days, but it was the only time I had the chance to interact with anyone at all. The whole time, little did they know I was sending packages filled with illegal substances.

We Know Love Best When Love is Lost

I would cry some days thinking about my family. Moments in and out of everyday would remind me of Kevin from Home Alone. I felt a survival response come out of me in the ways my mind would hold onto anything from the past that resembled love at all. Regret. Sympathy. Everything that once existed came to life and I would would write letters everyday. To my mom. To my dad. My gram. To the ocean. To the person I almost had an interaction with. When you're so alone like that the ways natural beauty becomes what you are grateful for. It reminded me maybe of what indians saw. Or maybe that's our perception of how we interpret what indians saw. The world and how they viewed the things around them. It was simple, but it was painful

I remember vividly, the way the ocean would come to life just to speak to me when I was sad. The way the waves would crash on an empty beach on a November day. That was the ocean's heartbeat to me, and it always calmed mine the ways it's body would travel to the horizon to meet the sky. Or maybe that's just what I believed to get through the days. I'd watch the sun and moon chase each other across the sky, and at night I'd walk to the pier of rocks where the ocean met the bay. I'd straddle my footsteps on the edge of water and sand and listen to the ways the stars on the west would whisper to the man made lights to the east of me. Some nights when the tide was low, my footsteps, too and from almost looked as if I wasn't alone. The ocean's heart beat creeping up to my feet to let me know I was safe. The stars painted across the sky reminded me like I was in my very own snowglobe. Looking back, I can see the ways I created any reason at all to be grateful. In the absence of, I think that is where our soul dies. Or maybe the opposite, the first time I learned to love beauty that I could not see before.

Day after day, each one just the same. I watched the deception from the barrier the internet would create as people from back home would be jealous of the pictures of where I called home. It didn't matter what I said, their responses only revealed their underlying values and it brought to life the ignorance in perception. I wanted more than anything for anyone to understand my pain. I took my sadness and tried my best to tie together beauty in depth in a manner that only showed me it never really mattered how we expressed ourselves, because people can only perceive based off of what they value. Little did they know how sad and alone I was. 20 years old, living alone just steps from the gulf of Mexico. It brought a sadness to life I wouldn't want anyone to ever feel. The shame and embarrassment that I felt. All i longed for was my family. Even a friend. and yet, all it took was the kindness of a cashier for me to be grateful for. I remember one time I called the number a buddy had given me, telling me to text when I felt alone and needed company. I did not know that number would lead to a prostitute sitting on the edge of my bed. I remember feeling no different than the same fear and panic of when I would try to hide behind my mothers legs as a child when she made me introduce myself to strangers. I watched her pull a bag of white powder out of her purse and she asked me for a spoon. She dumped the powder onto the spoon with a little bit of water, and drew the concoction up into a syringe. I watched her put the needle into the vein in the top of her hand. I sat on the bed paralyzed, feeling like I was going to have a heart attack. I don't know why I did it, but I remember just sprinting out the door. And I just ran. I didn't know where I was going and I don't remember what was going through my mind. All i remember is when I stopped, my heart was perfectly calm, and I was three miles away from my apartment. I crossed the ghostly streets and made my way a few blocks over to the beach. I straddled where the waves crashed into the sand, no different than the way I'd walk to the pier, until I found myself back at my place. I tucked into a ball and cried until I fell asleep. I wanted my family. One of the many times I experienced a panic attack before I ever knew what a panic attack even was.

It's on Us to be Grateful for Second Chances

The next trip home was like a new chapter had begun in the relationship that I had with my parents. I had never been so happy and grateful, and never before was I able to really talk to them, and I can only say that looking in hindsight. Of course I talked to them before that, but this time was different. Almost as if I was able to express the excitement in my emotion in a calm way that let me have more "normal" conversations with them. Before this, my relationship with them kinda reminded of the relationship that I had with Jake. I was always comfortable being quiet by their side, but now I felt as if I was able to be more myself. Whatever that meant.

I said before, the day Dom reached out to me was the day that changed my life forever. And this is where that spiral started to take place. Another season had passed and It was December 2012, tourist season was already over. Jake had made a friend from the bars that he liked to hook up with steroids. I gave him a price and product that he wasn't going to find anywhere else and I didn't mind helping him out.

It wasn't anything that I told Dom about but it honestly wasn't enough that Dom would ever know or be able to tell. My best friend who was a captain on the water, his girlfriend worked in a salon with the friend of Jake's and he told me that he had gotten in trouble for selling steroids before, and just to be careful. Things started getting weird after that because we hadn't heard from Jake's friend. I ended up driving home and it was three days after I had gotten home that I found out that the feds had raided both mine and Jake's places. I had moved in with some friends who worked on the water at this point and everyone thought I had ratted them out. It turned out, Jake had been selling the gear to an undercover informant. Being the new kids on the block, we were clueless. I remember the call the night I found out, my heart beating the same way as when that prostitute sat next to me on my bed. And being back home, I couldn't tell a soul. I panicked for a few days but I decided to try to enroll back in college. And I did....

Things were going okay! They were actually kind of good. I was excelling academically in ways that I didn't when I tried to go to college right out of high school. I was enjoying learning, and participating in class. It was something that I looked forward too, waiting for the professor to discuss something that I had a thorough understanding of. It was like a second chance, exactly the opposite from the first time I went to college, five years before.

It was the Friday night after valentines day and I was getting into my car to drive to the gym. I see a car pull up behind me and the cop lights start flashing. Sixteen US Marshalls surrounded me. Turns out, it was one of the biggest steroid busts in Florida history. The news article was a joke though, written in a way to make it out as if the supplements were unsafe for those who bought them. We knew it was just the spin for anyone reading to have second guesses, but it didn't matter at that point. Just like that, I was thrown in jail at the local state university. I was wanted from Florida and they legally had 90 days to come get me.

Jail wasn't that awful honestly. It took away the concern for all things petty we waste time on in our everyday free lives. All I did was write and workout. I was naturally kind and considerate. I never walked with a chip on my shoulder and I wasn't afraid either. I woke up early for first meal with everyone on the block. I'd workout afterwards doing burpees and pushups. The best workout was after supper though when I could get coffee packets from anyone who was going to throw them away. I don't think it'd be the same if I was there now though, I was so much stronger and more brave when I was young. Maybe thats what life does, it beats you down. Makes you question everything you believe. The corrections officers would always tell me how I didn't belong there. I was too polite to be in jail they said. I can thank my mother for that. Growing up an orphan I can see the ways she was so adament about what she instilled in me. It was what she knew of survival. Days went by and eventually I had the whole block working out. It was routine that the white inmates would workout at one time of the day. The black inmates at another. And the hispanic inmates at another time. The last few weeks there, the leaders of each group would workout with me through the day, all together. I'm not sure what that means, but it felt good. And it was a distinct movement within the block that everyone including the officers respected. People come from all walks of life in jail, and everyone wears a mask, portraying to be something harder than what they are. But it was a feeling I had never experienced before to understand and get along with someone in such close quarters, that came from a different world than you. But even with the masks people wear, you can still see the goodness in people who have experienced passion. love. loss.

I spent 87 days in jail before they finally came to expedite me. At first, it was a relief from the monotony of the every day routine. The same cell. The same table. The same tv for everyone to watch. The next four days would be just as shitty as my entire time in that jail. Expediting is what happens when criminals are wanted by another state. Since it was Florida that was after me, turns out I wasn't the only one that they wanted. We were cuffed by the hands and feet and thrown in the back of an extended van. It wasn't seated like you would think of in an SUV though, more like benches along each side, and we were packed tight. We went from Pennsylvania over to New Jersey. Then to New York. Indiana. West Virginia. South Carolina. Alabama. We'd stop twice at day at midnight and noon where we'd get a mcdonalds biscuit and a cup of water. The worst part was never knowing where we were going next. And when it got dark. It was pitch black and the only light was through a small hole in the middle of what separated us from the drivers. The moans and screaming at night from the inmates who would mentally break. The smell of piss. There was another person I'll never forget as long as I live. He had a swastica on his neck and he told me he accidentally killed a man in a race riot. Most things you hear from inmates are lies. Weak, cowardly people projecting a fascade to appear tougher from their weak nature. He was not one of them. He talked with passion, and that passion is what he believed in. "I've lived long enough to know not all black men are bad. But when it's time to riot with my people, I stand in the front." But he did not mind that I was not white. He felt like the closest thing to a friend I had had in a long time. And when we finally got to Florida, he stayed by my side. I was only there for two days though and I was out. Such an experience for something I should have been in and out for.

We are what we believe

We don't learn about insecurities until we grow in ways to understand that we aren't good enough. It doesn't mean what we believe is right, but the majority of what we believe in each chapter is altered from the beginning of our time, slowly until we accept what we call reality. Insecurities might be the downfall of the modern man. I don't think in any past chapter on the timeline did people struggle with insecurities like they do today. This right here might be the beginning of understanding something more about ourselves to help us lead better lives for the future. At the beginning of time, to be insecure was to lack security in surviving. And no longer are times like that. We've grown to where we compare ourselves to the person next to us. How sad that as we age this become instinctive to how we live. The psychological implosion be the downfall of man. Or the deception of who we believe we need to be. Or maybe that's just me.

As I get older the more I realize the gift we have is during the most vulnerable times of our lives. I think it's sad though, we're never able to realize that until it's too late. I don't know of any person who didn't wish to be older when they were a child. The only true way to appreciate that is to truly be grateful and present in the moment. I guess that's no different than being older though, and as contradicting as it may be, the real gift be in the naivety of our adolescents. Before we're able to understand feelings. Before we're able to even have those feelings, really. The ability to feel, itself, is something that evolves as we experience life.

Love doesn't come until after peace. But at the very beginning, it's love that creates peace for us, before we're even aware.. and maybe that's why the road to understanding is so difficult, because of the way our pasts are distorted through the false perception of our lens. Until we're forced to dissect it. Until we hurt enough alone that we have to cross paths with that...maybe

I wouldn't say I believe in religion, but I need God with all my heart. I suppose my need for him wouldn't come until after life would break me down though. If only I could have had him all my life. To think of jesus being in my heart as a child is no different than accepting something blindly.We have to fully believe, and that is not something I was capable of until I was broken down and saw for myself the ways we need jesus. But maybe that's because jesus was not in my home. And the contradiction of life, because everyone believed in God when I was a kid. I said I believed in God. But he was not in our home, even though anyone in my household would say they they believed in God as well. I suppose that surfaces the ignorance and betrayal of how we claim things blindly without truth in our heart. All of the cities I lived, and all of the ways I struggled, none of those things or places would have existed if God was in my heart. And to think back and remember times I said I believed in God as a child. It brings to life the difference between the things we say and the things that are in our hearts. The constant contradiction until we grow into who it is we are forever. A belief is not safe unless it is tested. Otherwise, we never really know what it is we claim until we experience life firsthand.

Time

There was a time when man used the sun's light to gather whatever was needed to provide for their familiy. I think we take the present moment for granted in alot of the freedoms we have. Or maybe that be something we should be more proud of, the evolution of where man has come from. Sometimes those men would not come home. And sometimes they came home with less than what was needed. The outcome of these times created enough remorse within the day to create passion towards the ones we love and protect. The principles that are instilled in our heart of what we witness before we're ever really paying attention. But at one time on the timeline, the equation of resources was close enough to survival to keep us honoring what we believed. And when what we believe revolves around the actuality of survival, love becomes our religion. And those closest to us are on the outward expression of how religion comes to life, before its anything we're even taught. I see it all around me in american culture, honor is dying, as we no longer have a respect for death. When we were concerned with survival from day to day, it created an urgency, as well as an appreciation for the very things we take for granted now. Survival gave us time. Time to ourselves. Time, where fear was no longer a part of the equation. And naturally we chased progression. That sums up our own greed, and perhaps the downfall of man as well. There was never a time where we were truly just content with being alive in the present moment. We live in a time where the greed and ignorance is outwardly showing in the hollow we become as humans.

Ignorance

I can remember when I was younger, the fear I had when my mother would make me introduce myself to her customers. The intense panic inside of me would paralyze me, I'd tremble trying to hide behind her legs. Growing up as an orphan in american culture was not easy. Growing up as an orphan anywhere is not easy. The value of parenting came to life the older I got and the more I realized I was raised to respect others, not to integrate into whatever this societal dynamic that make up American Culture be. But when you're by yourself, you also don't know how strong you are capable of being. Until that point, everything is in our mind. We project pain. sorrow. sympathy. Based off how reactions are inherited as the norm as we grow. The false perception we have of the world around us. I'm learning as I get older that this ignorance is what creates our peace as we age, the ability to hold onto the things we believe. The natural flaw we have, comes out as ignorance as we blame whatever unfulfilled inside our heart on what we perceive to be the cause. I watched my mother do this all her life. Everything unfulfilled in her life she would blame on never having parents. It wasn't until after she connected with her bloodline that she was finally able to find some closure. But that closure also came with the realization of the ways she built and chased an entire life around the ignorance of what survival made her believe. When I said God wasn't in my home as a child, that's because it was filled with her beliefs. From an early age, no woman would ever want to be with me if I did not have money. That was my religion. That is what she would constantly remind me of when she felt the panic of not having enough. We moved a dozen times before I even graduated high school. I was surviving long before I knew what survival was myself. That's because I inherited my mother's flaws before she was grown. I remember when it was her and I against the world, too. I remember moving from couch to couch, never really knowing who my family was. I never met my real dad. I remember the abusive one that came after though. Then the one where I learned about love by the one who would adopt me. And then the one she left him for with money. How sad is it to not know the difference between love and security. But what we believe ultimately grows into our reality as who she married the second time for security, was the one she fell in love with. But that is the one that would betray her, and bring what seemed like karma to life.

The best years of my life were the years I had a chance to feel what it was like to be part of a family. Such a short window of time, but it lives vividly in my heart and how life has shaped me. Looking back, I can see the ways I grew because I had never really witnessed love in a way up until this point. And to this day, anytime I think about going home, it's not a location, but this time period. My mother worked two jobs to give me a life she wish she would have had. She never let me forget that either, and she would always take her frustration out on one of us. She left my step dad because she grew unhappy with how much she worked. Looking back, I think she grew unhappy trying to fulfill her perception of what a family should have been.

without ever having a family I can see the ways her perception was flawed. I think we would have been happy with alot less too. THe expectations she placed on herself to give us all things we didn't need. In hindsight, I would have traded all the things I didn't need to not have to grow up walking on egg shells. He didn't make enough money to make her happy. Well, I take that back. I remember her being happy, but her perception of survival and how she was reminded of it too often to ever feel safe. And that's what makes me sad is that happiness is left because security is not present. When ultimately what creates love should be the ability to endure hard times together. That changed my father. In ways no one will ever know or see but me. She left my real father for the same reasons. I never met him but I can recall the stories she'd tell throughout my life of the ways he would gamble money away. The man after my father made lots of money, but I think she learned being beat and afraid was not worth the security. I didn't realize the ways the things we suppress and cover as we age would affect us as we grew older though. The memories, as scenes before I could really talk, of the extremity of emotion. It registers as fear and survival in my memories, the images of my mother screaming for me to hide. I'll always remember the look of fear as she tried to get away from him. and the blurry scenes shortly after of him picking me up from under the bed. It wasn't pain I remember, it was fear. The ways fear and panic before I even knew what fear and panic were, sculpted the rest of my life. THe ways we naturally gravitate and avoid scenes that have the potential to emulate that internal combination of chemistry that we register as panic and fear. And that be something that's different from person to person. I've grown to stay away from thoughts like these as they always end up with me sliding back into consciousness, sobbing on the floor. Tucked up in a bawl.

I had the chance to see a psychiatrist for a short period of time. In hindsight, I wish I had them all my life. They made me understand the ways I break down and fear loud noises and screaming because of this. Something that has always scared me is when people yell in an aggressive manner. THe emotions that I feel would ruin a normal person's day, be just as casual as filling a glass of water to me. I think the shame I felt deep down is what always made me feel inferior, anywhere I would go. Knowing deep down that the emotions I experienced were not what grown men were supposed to feel. That I did not grow into the man I was supposed too, and the ways that crumbled how I viewed myself. I used to think that chasing my dreams would give me this fulfillment of who I wanted to be. If I could bring my dreams to life maybe it would make up for the ways I was inferior. That thought only tells me how naive I really was. The hundreds of times i'd lose control and fall to the ground tucked up in a ball, hyperventilating with tears. Not something I like to bring up very often, but something that makes me sad as I learn to accept the harsh reality life is. It didn't have to be like this. Embarrassing really. Ashamed. No matter how much I tell myslef, " it wasn't your fault." It doesn't really matter, because it's still me on the floor, bawling. As a young child. In my teens. twenties....and now...

something about the ways people in america project empathy and sadness to the people of poor countries around the world. We feel bad, but that only reveals our ignorance in how we would feel in other people's situations. As I've gotten older I've seen this to be the way organizations create scams, using people's empathy against them. Sometimes I think church be no different, but I always ask for forgiveness when ugly thoughts like that cross my mind. That's something I've learned as I've gotten older, the way we speak of anything beyond ourselves can only reveal where our own ignorance lies. I always catch myself thinking, you can tell the most about people by listening to what they complain about. The level of depth and adversity, and it usually just leaves me envious. To wish my life had unraveled in a way that these are things I would get upset about. LIfe has taught me that as long as we live, we can only grow, no matter how broken we are. Time really does heal all. It's gotten to the point, where it is not life that causes the extremes of chemical reactions in my body that outwardly come out as feelings; but people. The fear and unknown surrounding how we cross paths with other humans, their motives and intent something that is never blatant or on the surface. I imagine at one point on the timeline during a much more primitive age, crossing paths with another human was dangerous, and in my mind I have to remind myself not to naturally think these ways. In the chapters I've had more structured purpose, I wasnt always this afraid. I guess it comes from learning that people from all walks of life are capable of anything. Through the right lens, I be the bad guy in a persons story too. Early on, we learn to associate looks with types of people. The way they're dressed. How they carry themselves. And then as you age you realize the ignorance in judging a book by its cover. But there still holds some truth to this, but not enough you can ever rely on its accuracy.

New Chapter

I feel that panic now. I guess you could say I've been in a constant state of panic now for six months or so. I'm grateful in the moments that come by where I can just be present in the moment. Not having the stability of a home makes me feel like a stray animal. Without the love of the parents that guide us, I only grow to feel more ashamed and the way that isolates me more and more. What makes it even more difficult is looking at the ways I made money in the past. Somewhere along the timeline though, I made a promise to myself to be good. I think I had to lose everything for that too happen though. When I was so broken and alone, feeling like a child left to die. That's when I knew I needed God. That I did not have the answers. And looking back, my stepfather was the introduction of love in my life as a child. But to see the ways it guided and helped me grow. When my mother left my father, I saw those very traits of instability outwardly surface as high school became dark and lonely for me. In ways I did not know though, I would try to connect with words but I did not have the vocabulary or understanding to express myself authentically. In the same ways I see the rest of the world around me now. Paralyzed by the contradiction of their lives, but without the understanding of truth in actuality to be able to articulate what it is they feel inside. All the things that make up the construct of how we believe life to be, those are the very things that need to be tested for us to witness in order to believe full heartedly. I remember crying alot. And I say that now, but those tears were alone throughout every chapter of my life. I learned how to fit in. I thank my mother for that as well, growing up being so concerned with the opinions and thoughts of how we are viewed. Or maybe because we were vietnamese in a small ignorant town of vietnam veterans. I struggled with depression before I knew what depression was. I remember any conversation I had with my mother just ended up her scolding me for the ways I needed to grow. Who I needed to be. What I needed to be doing. And I know those are important things, but times in my life I just wanted my mother too. I eventually shut off and went mute. I wouldnt' speak, only one word answers. and looking back some teachers saw and sympathized, but my walls were so high I could only recognize that they felt for me. Growing up where I'm from is not a place where children are raised to speak of their feelings.

The Present

I'm not really sure how I got here. I had grown into the man I always wanted to be, and after I had learned about being on the spectrum of autistism, everything kind of spiraled apart, and no one was there. It turns out, I had only grown in ways from the love that was instilled in past chapters. Learning about autism helped me understand all the turns and curves in my life in ways that I had never seen before. I keep having these visions of the military in and out of my days. I can't really explain it, other than I feel protected. Is that where I'm supposed to be? It makes me wonder if there was more to my mother's story than what we know. Who was it that brought her here. What did her father do in the army? What was he doing in Vietnam? To only be a fly on the wall in his time serving in my mother's native land, but those decades have past.

Growing up, I viewed myself no different than all the other white kids at recess. But more than ever, I can't help but think there's a story to my bloodline that I need to know. My mother was brought here as an orphan, and most of our life I took on her struggles of never meeting her parents. The emptiness that left her to survive all of her life. She had never had a family. She had never even seen what love is, and there are times I used to want to be mad at her because I know the only thing that kept her going was having me. She should not have been a mother, and when I catch these thoughts running through my mind it's just a matter of time before I feel the cold in my veins, and the goosebumps on my arms. And after a few minutes I pick myself up and dry my cheeks off and continue with my life. I would only learn these lessons by learning to describe what it is I yearned for as I got older. Because they were all the things my mother had never experienced. I ask for forgiveness when I have thoughts of blaming her though. No different than when I have thoughts that question God's intent. I apologize in my mind and move on trying not to bother anyone. The last time we spoke she had told me how much joy she had being my mother. And when I got too expensive that I had to go. Those were the underlying beliefs she had as a mother. When I think of that I wish she never would have had me at all. I remember her telling me stories about her 3rd or 4th foster family, being dropped off at a bus station with a bag of clothes and 20$. She stood there for 8 hours until a cop picked her up and took her to the shelter. That makes me cry too....

To find out there was an entire bloodline that existed here in the united states, when all along we were left to believe it was her and I by ourselves. In a poverty stricken town made up of Vietnam Veterans. And how much pain that's caused us through the years. How much she hurt all those years. And now the domino effect of repercussions because of the beliefs we grew up believing.

I thought it was a sign when Bill was brought into my life. Shortly after my mother connected with the bloodline she never knew she had, Bill gave me what I thought was the gift of a new life. He had built a community center in my hometown and I volunteered to coach his son who was playing college football. I was thankful during covid that he allowed me to use the facility while everything was shut down. I would stay after I trained his son and I couldn't have been more grateful to have that. Training had always been a deeper part of my life, and the older I got, the more I realized in ways I did not know. He gave me a home, and a chance at a new life, and I remember how excited I was, being so afraid I would never have a home. It didn't take long to realize the reasons I never did though. Over and over again I would convince myself the things I needed to do, but being totally alone it was almost as if my body was following a different autopilot that I could not control. The only sense I can make of it was that it reminded me of something more primal. More primitive. Unless it struck me having to do with survival, no matter how hard I tried, I could not bring myself to do the things that I needed to do. I'd listen to the patterns of the neighbors and how they'd mow their lawns on friday mornings. The consistent decibal levels that would register in the short time I was there. It seemed silly to me to spend time in a calculated way cutting the grass that didn't even need to be cut. The more I was there the more I saw how unfit I was to be taking care of a home by myself. I turned into a monster half the time, training in the basement. I didn't have much but it was such a peaceful flow in the ways I would make my heart beat. All I had to do was prop my phone against a gatorade bottle and record my natural flow. that was enough to entertain my audience in ways that I could talk about fitness. training. life. methods. love. all to generate just enough revenue to make ends meet. And that was enough for me. I tried, over and over again, anytime I had a surplus of money saved, the will to do these things that I didn't want to do would die. And as much as it sounds like an excuse I watched myself through these same patterns over and over and over.

I was always excited to hear from Bill, helping him on his deer farm was something I enjoyed. He did not know how alone I truly was though, otherwise I don't think he would have done what he did. When I wasn't training, I would take my paddleboard to the state park, a natural beach tucked away in the mountain. I remember the ways my heart would calm as I turned off the dirt road and I'd lose all service. I thought that the lonliest days of my life were in the past. A chapter of my life I associated with a less mature and naive version of myself. I had the things I feared all my life, I was the exact man I had always wanted to be, and yet, I never felt more alone or inadequate as a man. Visions of Florida would always run through my mind, reminding me of this exact feeling. Al those lonely nights I'd spend walking the shoreline, the only person in existence for the moon to watch over...

I contemplated the idea of a life without romance. Moments I would trade it for the love I came from. Who I would call a brother, both of our parents were brought here from asia during the war. He had a beautiful family, a wife and three girls, and a newborn son. They were special. In all my life, how rare it was to see children raised off love, not off a societal norm. They didn't care about money or things I was told to believe in growing up. And his girls all shined because of it. They were proof, what I always believed, and how they thrived in all aspects of life, school, and they filled my heart everyday feeling like a big uncle to a family I never had. I had a mattress on the corner of the floor in a small room by myself, and it was more than enough because I was happy for the first time in my life, and yet I continued to chase what I was told to believe. Looking back, the answers were there all along in the authenticity of the things I felt. We are not always open to understanding our feelings and where they come from and that is what will cause the majority of our pain in life. Making decisions with a lesser known understanding of what we feel is best for us, based off what we grew up believing was best for us. Those are what I call chains, and not everyone has them, and not always are they clear to see. But it's important for those who wear them to recognize the pain that is not needed because of how the past still haunts us...

I did not know however, that that life would be taken from me, just to remind me of my inadequacies as a human. My inability to support myself. The equation to exist on our own regardless of how "high functioning" will never be the goal. The goal to sustain life by one's self under the spectrum of autism is only to fade towards the ending without love. We need Love. Love drives everything in and out of what we do. We can not exist without love, and that presents itself as family, as value, as beliefs, in and out of each chapter.

Ten days before christmas Bill told me that he was sorry but I needed to find somewhere else to go and he wanted to sell the house. I had volunteered to run a barbell club at his community center for almost a year. I thought that I could use that environment to capture enough content that I would need to post online to advertise and create revenue. Coming from the poorest area in the state, people were not so concerned with fitness or health though. It was an eye opener for me. When I had grown into the man that I wanted to be. And when I say that, the moral compass that guides us internally in ways no one knows but ourselves. The deep secrets of how our mind works. I had gone through chapters where I am not proud of the person I had been, but this growth was something sincere. I felt it, and when I did, I believed I could move back to the place I called home to make it. I was wrong, and I regret leaving vegas so soon. I had started traveling over the mountain to a more populated area because fitness was something more common.

The melting pot of the university being one of the most prestigious international universities in the world created an energjy that made me feel not like an outcast. A friend of mine helped me find a psychiatrist that would work with me without having insurance. It's then that I found out about being on the spectrum of autism. The technical term is called Aspergers, but they had removed that from the DSM, the book that classifies all mental health disorders. So now, the term is just considered "the spectrum of autism". Learning about this at first was kind of relieving. It made sense out of so much of my past and the decisions I made where I wish I would have had more support. Each one of those six cities didn't have to exist, but on my own without any support, I can see the ways I panicked inside. How it was fear and survival instinct that drove each of those cities to exist at all. But I always created some sort of success wherever it was I was going. This was a little different now, a brand new environment and I could see all the autistic traits within myself in every new scenario. Imagine not being able to walk, because it's no longer a natural movement. What to do with our hands. When the speed of thought travels faster than the body's movements, I could feel the glitch in what was considered natural to now be difficult. The inability to make eye contact with anyone because of the ways my mind raced around other humans. It wasn't always the case though, if we somehow found ourselves on a topic I understood, I had to remind myself not to stare into someones eyes too long when I get excited. Part of it makes me grateful that I've had the experiences I have in my life. I was always a little awkward, but being such an exceptional athlete all my life is something that kinda kept me in the "cool kids" group. Not that I ever felt that I belonged, but it's just how it was. It gave me enough experience from city to city to kind of be able to blend in. But if I thought too much about any of it, my mind would just create patterns out of all the places I've been. The ways when people are around me, I don't think that I see what people see. Most people are so self absorbed to notice anything other than the way they wish to be perceived. I noticed the colors and sounds first. And then the speed of how those colors move around me. The urgency and obnoxious movements are the ones I automatically tune out. If I don't have purpose to wherever it is I am, the conversations all around me, blend with the noise of the environment, and the colors and movements come to life in what I would say resemble what soundwaves look like when a person is playing music. People never understood that if I was in public with them, how valuable they are to me. because of the ways I choose to pay 100% attention on them. They're my rocks, that protect me from the sounds coming to life too much. It sounds crazy, imagine a side walk full of people. and you see me tucked into the closest corner I can find. My arms around my knees, rocking, focused on my breathing. Otherwise it's just tears. What makes me sad is that no one understands. Not a soul. And the person I wanted to understand the most was the first person I ever truly believed in my heart I could spend forever with. I had a few serious relationships up until this point, and they taught me more than I could ever imagine by myself. When we dissect the raw truth of our thoughts to understand what drives our motives. Most people will never understand how selfish and ignorant they really are. But sometimes I feel that's what makes the world go round. The majority of people will never be able to see the things they dream in such a real light to understand why it was they dream these things at all. If there was anything I think the people should have, it's the ability to experience the things they dream and wish deep down. Most people never have the courage to tip toe in that direction because of the ways it makes us vulnerable, but if they did, and somehow they managed to chase those dreams down, they would see that the grass is not greener on the other side. Dreams are merely an ignorant projection of a reality that we believe would somehow fulfill our quality of life. I watch people all around me with impure thoughts and dreams when in reality, they don't realize that everything that fills their heart is right in front of them. Dreaming is something I've learned that comes when we're protected and surrounded by love. Love is what gives us the strength to dream in ways most of us will never realize. The natural contradiction that life be, in the ways we grow to fulfill what it is we always believed growing up we were supposed to be. The saddest thing is to live a life and get to a point where we understand everything we did was because of what someone wanted us to do. And when we realize this, the web we've woven of life, I hope is not so deep that you can't get back what's genuine in your heart.

Everyday I'm reminded I don't belong here. the plate of cooked beef patties on the table, for days as I slowly graze at it in passing. In my mind I feel like I should be wandering on sand or under trees in some place less primitive and far away. The more time I spend alone the more time I see these traits surface that make me worry my time is running out. I cry through the days when I'm reminded how I've ended up all alone. That's not something I would tell anyone though, I know that's not acceptable and frowned upon. And honestly, it doesn't even bother me. I cry. I let the tears fall. And I move one with my day. It's not that I'm alone, it's that I experienced the love I had always dreamed and lost those moments in the mistakes I didn't know I was making trying to be better. I used to think I was just sensitive, but now it's gone too far, I can't help but be ashamed at whatever is wrong with me.

Bill had moved to my hometown before I had ever knew he existed. He had used his knowledge of oil and land against confidential information to make lot's of money. I helped him on his deer farm when he asked, and learning from him was the closest thing I had to a father since I was a child. Learning from him was honestly the most amount of interaction I had at all. He made me feel safe, and I trusted him. He would say things like " one day when I'm at your wedding," and made me feel like I had a life long friend. He gave me a home. He made me feel protected. When I started traveling to try to find more work, it wasn't long before he told me I needed to find somewhere else to live. He wanted to sell the home. At this point, I had built so many walls and grew so much in isolation, if

I had a problem I honestly didn't have a soul to call. The woman I said I wanted to spend forever with. THe pressure of moving in was too much. But I can't blame her. The panic and the urgency it brought out in me. I was better off alone, my problems were too much for anyone I cared about. And if I cared about them, I depended on them. But i understand I will be alone until I learn to grow in ways normal people do. And that's what I've learned the most. The more inadequate I felt, the more I hid myself from the people I needed all along. To the point where I was left alone. Imagine being so sad and alone that the highlight of your days was the kindness of the grocery store cashier. Or the random acts of kindness youd look for in any natural interaction. I called those jesus moments. I found myself panicking not knowing what to do or where to go. I'd do anything to make these anxious feelings go away. THe more alone I was, the more I felt inferior to kids half my age. I admired and looked up to every single college student. To be at the prime of their life and to be able to decide what they get to learn about that sets them up for the rest of their lives. I was envious of every single one. I always caught myself thanking kids that were kind to me. I'm not sure if that's an autistic trait or not, but it made me feel like it was something that jesus would smile at.

I had moved in with a friend I had met recently. Mostly because I didn't have any other options, and this was the first time I had really spent close time with anyone at all. He was in his last semester as an engineering student from Saudi Arabia. And he was the most simple and kind hearted human, I had never wished the best for anyone like I did him. I was sad when he finished school, but was so excited for him. He had grown depressed here, I think because of the culture barriers, but to me he was no different than how I would view someone who was white. Now im here all by myself again and I need to find a new place to live soon and I'm not sure where to go. This makes me wish the military could adopt me. Or maybe even the university. I would do anything to feel safe. To have purpose. When I'm afraid all the time it makes me lock up and I'm reminded of those autistic traits. From my experiences though, from practicing writing all those years. I had the ability to open up to people, but it was a very select environment with delicate variables that would allow that. I like it better when I can talk and be excited around people. And now I've built so many walls I don't know how to get that back.

We Need Solitude, But Not too Much

Most people never find themselves totally alone in life. And when I say totally alone, I don't mean just lonely for a weekend with nothing to do. I don't mean no social interactions outside of work or family. I mean totally alone. From an early age we naturally move in ways to prevent that from happening. We don't really understand the motives behind the ways we move until everything is taken away from you. And even then, I would say it's not something we understand. Because sitting alone with the uncertainty of our thoughts is not something anyone favors. We have to start from scratch, over and over again until we start to understand how we build habits within our routines to accommodate our needs.

the 90s will truly serve as a special era of existence. Most of my adult life I always thought that was true, but the older I get the more I understand why. The demographic of people who saw a way of life before the virtual world took over. Some of my earliest memories were using the computer at night. When I think of what we used them for, it wasn't anything to the degree it is today. Seeing the evolution of technology and how it serves us. Ultimately was the turning point in the evolution for man, quickly turned into the downfall of man. And that time accelerated when the virtual world was created. We did not know it would lead to the downfall of man, where it is no longer the fear of death, but the fear of judgement, from those whose judgement we value. And the thing about that, is that we will trace through time to find how that was planted inside us, as a belief, as our own religion in what was the underlying root to how we would move through life.

When it comes to survival, most animals in the wild will be in danger at least once through the day. and always the alertness of safety through the night. This affects the way we let outsiders inside our walls. No longer is survival a daily thought among american culture. When we're younger, the survival response takes place through the majority of toddler years. Earning trust. Communicating through emotion, the bond of influence and the impact that has through the most influential years of imprinting. Those things come to life as lessons inside me the more I feel the extent of alone and sadness as a man. It wasn't always understanding in the moment to give us the answers we needed. Sometimes life had unravel and happen enough for us to be able to compare why we did the things we did, because of how we were influenced, and what it was we valued. All things protected in ways they'll never know, the love we have we'll never see. Until its too late, and we learn because of the way the present hurts without it. The chapters that go by that pain still linger, correlate to the regret of the mistakes we didn't know we were making.

When I think of Jesus' word, the ways those words come to life the more I spend time in solitude. The understanding of his literal meaning, combined with metaphoric analogies, and the possibility that your perception is on the spectrum of accurate. In any given moment.

Regardless of the household you grew in, where you grew will impact how you learn.

When love is fulfilled, the heart is full and so the presence of it requires a process to be earned. The ability for that to happen takes place during the youthful years you spend with your peers, before the words laws of attraction have any value to you, but the little by little each day in the impact of connection you gradually make with those around you. as you age the projection of your immediate future is laid out, and in those environments will be variables and ideas that have the ability to earn influence over you, in the ways your heart opens up to them. Once we are old enough to have established friendships with our peers, the values of influence are divided.

The progress of each nation with its own religion and the way we are growing to overlap with other nations and their beliefs if something I see unfolding. In such a way that bring world affairs together to align with the holy world. And now that we know, the money needs to flow as a resource in a manner that is justified, so the current events are aligning with the distribution of power by means of a narration of whatever justified. It wasn't always like this. At one point the events naturally occured. And now, war is what causes the biggest flow of money and the display of those wars is what is given to us as a whole to impact the influence it has on the direction people will move.

these are the visions that I cannot turn off. I've never had dreams before I came here. and I associate it with beauty, the thoughts they inspire and how that drives my body in a way I cannot control. I feel like an animal dying without sun or water. I catch myself saying I want to go home. Scanning for it in anything I can interpret, and the way Jesus' word grows in every scene I see.

In all the places I lived, I didn't know I was getting a first hand opportunity to experience the development of cultures around the major industrialization points that we call cities of the united states. I remember my freshman year of college. You could step right off campus and see the barbed wire along fences. Las vegas had some of the most beautiful architecture I've ever seen. The visuals of buildings that made up what they call sin city. But we should know from history that colonies don't blossom in the desert, they flourish where this is trees and water. My second year in college I transferred to smaller state university. I didn't tell anyone that I bought a one way ticket to puerto rico and dropped out. I'm not sure what I was thinking, in my mind I wanted to backpack around the island. Before I had dropped out I would run as the only way to calm my mind. Id run around the center of the town and pinpoint which buildings were historical based off their distance from the library. from the post office. from the town square. And to watch the evolution of building structures through the 17, 18, and 1900s. These are the visions I have been running from

I am the one who doesn't belong. and that makes me sad because of the mistakes i have made. To see people all around me who I could help with the knowledge that life has given me. But I am no one anymore. And If I have to go, I wouldn't want people to know at all. Just let me go and let them forget, because no would even know now.

In these times I feel like the end is near, love is all i can miss. But to miss it now would put me on my knees in a way I can not handle. To long for the woman you gave your heart too. It hurts to think of her presence, for her to argue my love for her. I wish I was better to even reach out. To reach out at my lowest is to know she deserves better. And I cannot give her that, but i know no man will love her like I do. Because she is the woman I saw forever with for the first time. The first time in my heart, deep down, I knew I loved her more than anything. The ways she made me change in ways noone would know but yourself.

It was a huge part of my life growing up, the emptiness of my mother being brought here as an orphan during the vietnam war. The life that would set her up to live. The abandonment. The loss. The lack of trust. In the wild it is true what they say, you cannot trust another human being, because we do not know when the intent is barbaric and less civilized. But I suppose that's something we learn as we grace the timeline. What we would associate with barbaric is no longer an accurate lens. The deception of actuality lies in our ignorance, or maybe the perception of portrayal, giving us truth to the rarity that is, of man's perception ever aligning with the actuality. Forever distorted.

Something my mother would always tell me about, what it was like when she was growing up. But she was raised in and out of foster care for the majority of her life. The only constant from the owner of a small chinese restaurant who was brought here with her during the war. The stories of ancestors hundreds of years ago. I would listen because I know my mothers heart was raised broken and I choose not to punish her for the ways it hurt me growing up. The things she instilled as a mother because of what surviving has taught her on her own. Those things would then hurt me as well, but if there is not change, then that is our flaw. and so we just keep those things quiet. like religion. safe, sacred

It's not that anyone ever wants to die. that couldn't be any further from the truth. The end of life only comes when hope is lost. The absence of love to save us, without direction. leaves us empty and alone in ways tomorrow has no light. In ways, what we hold onto from the past tears us apart as there is no reason for a future without what it is our heart yearns for. It's the process of love, and all it entails that unravels what it is we call of a life. At first, the love that raises us. The love that propels us. Motivates us. The pursuit of. The understanding of; all those things in constant motion as we let the world around us sculpt how it is we age.

Our lens for love is held to the underlying pursuit of freedom we never really verbalize we are on. When we realize the chains we wear without knowing, we understand the possibility of influence beyond our awareness. Our extent of freedom will dictate our lens for love. The chains we wear most closely related to the values we have. The idea of love, and that whatever it is we are after and the role it serves in our quality of life.

I sympathize for the future and all the ways our hearts will break. We've come to a point in existence where we are no longer good for ourselves. The silent wars each one of us will fight as we build a life we are told. And the pain will come in the ways as we slowly start to realize the discontent and sadness with the things that contradict what our heart is really after. It doesn't have to happen to those raised and protected by love throughout their life. It is those who go through chapters empty, banking on a path that was projected for them in an earlier life. The end result will be addiction. The decline of mental health. Crime. Betrayal. And in ways we won't even pay for until we realize the value of truth and goodness. And it takes being broken to understand, and by the time that happens, the things that will have broken us will distort the value of where these lessons come from. The best advice I could give is to understand what love is in any chapter, and live for it. I mean really live for it. Be wholesome and fierce in the ways we are vulnerable for what matters most.

I don't like it when I feel like this. The best way I can describe it is that it feels like there's an equation. Except there's no hope, and the walls are closing in. And in the moments I'm left with these thoughts, I guess these are the times I wish I had a family. Or even a friend. I guess I've gone long enough in solitude, is it too selfish to ask God for hope. I know that God hears those who need him though, it just makes me wonder what it is to need, to know the times I've been broken down.

The Way Love is Passed Down

I think of a child that cries, and the way a mother's love naturally dries the cheeks of where those tears look for life. The sympathy we show to even strangers, as crying be a universal symbol of pain. Hundreds of times a single thought will make my cheeks no different than that crying childs. There is no love to protect my cheeks like that mothers though. That seems like a fairytale, the thought of another human showing compassion in those times I cry. But I know that's not something that exists. Like a homeless man believing in santa clause, I've learned to just let those tears run their course. And in doing so, the walls that's built around me. If anything, we learn about ourselves in the moments of extreme emotion. Most of the time the feelings be accompanied by irrationality, and I've found most people just silently push to move on from times like those. But at the onset, there is always a thought process that's channeled back to passion. remorse. A trail of thoughts that connects us to emotions, if only we are patient enough to sit amidst what's overwhelming inside us.

Save the Children

As I've gotten older I've learned the value of what being a parent means. The role we play in how a child's heart grows and develops. Not only is it a combination of how that child views the world around them, but all the ways we're rubbing off on them in ways we don't even see. That was one of the biggest lessons I learned being a father. We're so busy being caught up in life, and then those moments that children remind us the beauty that exists in freedom. And before we know it, a lifetime goes by and we realize that children were the bridge all along. The bridge to understanding. and that being free and love were the answers the whole time.

It's important the example we set for our children. That sounds cliche and easy to agree with but we forget that the most important lessons are the ones where our patience is tested facing adversity for them to see. It's not just what we preach, it's what they see when they are watching us face the world too.

There's Beauty in Timing

God wasn't something that was introduced to my life until our family was falling apart. We turn to God when we are in pain and need him the most, but sometimes his answers are not when we'd like, but on his terms. I don't know how many times I've seen people move on, only for God to answer those prayers, and thinking we don't need him now, so we turn our back on him. And it's not that we mean to do that, it's that our eyes and heart are only open to him when we need him most. And that is something I have learned first hand. We want the struggle. Because that is God's way of testing us before he gives us all that we dream.

The only time I ever saw my dad cry was when my mother left him. I was just a boy, and I've learned we are incapable of understanding the extent of pain and emotion until we have felt it first hand. I remember the first night my mother left us. I listened to my father weep through the night praying to God. I prayed to God too. And it bothers me I cannot remember what I asked for specifically, but the significance of that defining moment, in ways I would continue to dissect for 20 years after. I did not understand then, only that crying was sad.I knew he was hurt, and I was hurt. And if only I could go back now to know the ways we would need each other.

The madness in my projection

The mood matters, and trust me, probably a decade I've tried to suppress the extent of how sensitive I am. That is something subjective from person to person though, the feelings they have, the extent of sadness, how much sadness, and the ways they are associated with the experiences of their life and what that outwardly looked like in a social dynamic. The correlation between feeling and experience and how that shapes how we grow with how we are taught to value those character traits. So when I say that mood matters, the sensitivity to how easily that mood can be affected, especially when the heart is attached to what fluctuates. That's the best way I can describe it. The greater the extent of whatever the specific mood, in times I feel inferior, the things that are not real become alive as feelings. The way a projected fear has the ability to come to life with the right mindset and variables. The older I get the more I see the ways it has kept me alone. The things I was neglected of not only set the standard for what I would chase, it set me up to chase what was not meant for me. I want to be mad. I do not know who to blame for this madness in my mind, to know there is potential for any good, in any way, but to feel inadequate as the walls around me close in such a way to make me feel like there is no room for me here. any town. any city. the beach, perhaps, but now I am too weak to find my way there.

Today, maybe

Life is taking the things you've learned all your life, and being able to understand the significance in each chapter of your life, how it unfolded, and the ways it shaped who we are today. And then when we learn of love in a new way, where what we've learned up until this point is no longer useful to the love we know now. We can now nurture the child to give the love we wish we would have had. But to serve love now is to grow in ways that challenge everything. Little does that boy know I am trying my best to overcome the walls I never knew I had. To know that my flaws now expose you to a type of love in nurturing that to take away from you is selfish of me. The greatest days of my life have been creating what a true home should look like for you, adoring the woman who learns of love raising you. From the ways I have seen what a broken home will do to a man. When that man was broken as a boy, because of the lack of stability in the love that nurtured how he grew.

Letters to the child we wonder if we'll see again

And as for love itself. The moments it feels like its falling apart, are the ways the toxic in each of us collides. The last bit of how we never had to grow. I can admit it is not either one of us alone, but the negative energy created when certain emotions inside us are unattended. I have watched the ways we've grown trying to save the chapters of us. To be able to recognize when things we don't mean come from a place where we can't navigate our differences. You know truth in love, when you see that it is not whether it's right or wrong, rational or not. It's because it is hers, and she is what you love. What we believe makes up the realities of how we view the world, and it is important to know this so that our flaws do not hurt in us in ways we don't deserve.

What we love, from what we learn in life, is different than what we love because of what we grow up believing we are supposed too. And sometimes that love is unspoken throughout those years to make it difficult to understand why we gravitate towards what we do at certain times. The very atmosphere of influence that makes up what inspires how you grow, is determined by your heart and the things in your world in ways before we're ever paying attention. There also comes a time when the love that we have learned of from living life on our own, that will conflict with the love that has guided us. No one teaches us about that, though. When it comes down to it, the most important thing we can do is protect the vision. Because when that vision falls apart and the present moment collides with what we always believed, chaos will begin. And in the scenario the love that guided us can no longer protect us, everything we believed up until this point could be broken. And in the wrong time of life, perhaps too much to want to move on. The beauty in timing exists, and it comes down to the ways we grow in and out of each chapter, pursuing the perception of love that has been instilled inside us. If this were the end, I'd want to say sorry to those that mattered before I learned to understand. And I'd want everyone to be brave now, to be courageous now, not for anything scary, but to say I love you in whatever the most genuine way possible. Find a way to do that over and over again, and the rest of life will fall into place.

The End